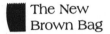

The New
Brown Bag

Touch the Water

The New
Brown Bag

Touch the Water

Phyllis Vos Wezeman
Anna L. Liechty
Kenneth R. Wezeman

THE
PILGRIM
PRESS
Cleveland

To Lief Daniel David Wezeman, our third grandson. May God's gift of water be a lifelong reminder of Jesus' love for you.

—P.V.W. AND K.R.W.

In memory of the Reverend Ray Hilty, pastor of Greenwood–Oak Park Community Church in Kettering, Ohio, whose loving guidance helped me confirm the baptism vows my parents made on my behalf.

—A.L.L.

The Pilgrim Press, 700 Prospect Avenue East
Cleveland, Ohio 44115-1100
pilgrimpress.com

© 2003 Phyllis Vos Wezeman, Anna L. Liechty, and Kenneth R. Wezeman

07 06 05 04 03   5 4 3 2 1

Library of Congress Cataloging-in-Publication Data

Wezeman, Phyllis Vos.
    Touch the water / Phyllis Vos Wezeman, Anna L. Liechty, Kenneth R. Wezeman.
       p.   cm.   (The new brown bag)
    ISBN 0-8298-1518-X (pbk. : alk. paper)
    1. Baptism—Sermons.   I. Liechty, Anna L.   II. Wezeman, Kenneth R.
  III. Title.   IV. Series

BV813.3.W49   2003
252'.53–dc21

                                                    2003043457

Contents

Introduction 7

Overview 8

1. Accepted by God: Cornelius's Baptism *Acts 10:1–48* 11

2. Called to Repentance: Jordan's Significance
   Matthew 3:1–6 13

3. Challenged to Remember: Christ's Sacrifice
   Mark 15:1–39 15

4. Changed by God: Paul's Conversion *Acts 9:1–20* 17

5. Cherished by God: Abraham's Covenant
   Genesis 17:1–7, 15–16 19

6. Claimed by God: Noah's Ark *Genesis 6:11–9:17* 21

7. Cleansed by God: Nicodemus's Lesson *John 3:1–21* 23

8. Commissioned by Christ: Disciples' Instructions
   Matthew 28:16–20 25

9. Confessed in Faith: Christ's Name *Philippians 2:9–11* 27

10. Confirmed in Faith: Our Promise *Ephesians 1:13–14* 29

11. Connected to God: Christ's Resurrection *Colossians 2:12* . . .32

12. Covered by Grace: Water's Message *Acts 8:26–40* 34

13. Dedicated to God: Love's Response *Luke 2:25–40* 36

14. Empowered for Ministry: Jesus' Baptism
    Matthew 3:13–17 38

15. Filled with the Spirit: Pentecost's Power *Acts 2:37–42* 40

16. Focused for Mission: Epiphany's Promise *John 1:29–34* 42

17. Gifted for Life: Baptism's Remembrance *John 14:13–14* 44

18. Guided in Life: Christ's Flock *John 10:14–15* 46

19. Nurtured in Faith: Infant Baptism
    Genesis 17:7; Psalm 22:9–10; Matthew 19:14 48

20. Promised in Faith: God's Covenant
    Jeremiah 31:31–34, Hebrews 8:10–12 50

21. Purchased with Love: Simon's Mistake *Acts 8:4–25* 53

22. Received in Faith: Lydia's Welcome *Acts 16:11–15* 55

23. Released from Sin: Jailer's Conversion *Acts 16:16–35* 57

24. Saved by Grace: Moses' Deliverance *Exodus 14:21–22* 59

25. Sealed in Baptism: Scripture's Instructions
    John 3:5; Ephesians 1:13 61

26. Summarized in Song: Jesus' Love *1 John 4:9–10* 63

27. Symbolized by Sacraments: God's Love
    Mark 16:15–16 65

28. Touched in Love: Jesus' Blessing *Mark 10:13–16* 67

29. United by Love: God's Children
    1 Corinthians 12:12–13 69

30. Welcomed in Faith: God's Family *Ephesians 3:14–15* 71

Age-Group Suggestions 73

Hymn Story Cross-References 77

Scripture Cross-References 79

Teaching Tool Cross-References 83

Theme Cross-References 85

Introduction

Baptism is one of the central practices of the Christian faith. Regardless of denomination, nationality, race, or theological position, all Christians practice baptism. Some Christians believe that only believers are to be baptized as children, youth, or adults; others baptize infants. Some use total immersion, many sprinkling, others pouring. In spite of differences, baptism helps to define us as followers of Jesus.

Christians baptize in response to the command of Jesus. It is the act by which God welcomes us into the church. We may be Christians when we believe in Jesus, but it is not until we are baptized that we receive our official welcome into the family of God. In that sense it is a little like graduation from high school or college. Before the graduation ceremony we complete all of the assignments and requirements. In a sense, we are finished with school. It is behind us, yet we are not graduates. It is not until we receive our diploma that we are graduates. Graduation is the sign that something has been accomplished and that a new stage of life has begun. Baptism is similar in a spiritual sense.

In the act of baptism God promises us that our sins are washed away; we are raised with Christ to new life and made members of God's family. God has accomplished something for us and now invites us to new life. Baptism marks and celebrates our new status. As you use this book to help others discover the significance of the sacrament in their lives, we invite you to celebrate your baptism and to remember that you are a child of God and a member of the family of faith.

Overview

What is this book?

Children's Sermons on Baptism is a collection of thirty messages primarily designed for kindergarten through upper-elementary youth. This resource addresses the sacrament of baptism from a variety of approaches. While each sermon is based on a scripture passage or verse, some lessons focus on biblical stories related to baptism; several explain contemporary and traditional hymns used during the sacrament; and others explore theological themes regarding the church's ancient rite of initiation.

Each message uses a consistent format based on the following components:

PASSAGE: Each sermon is based on a specific scripture text, which is listed for reference.

PURPOSE: Each message's central theme is summarized in one simple statement.

PREPARATION: A suggestion for a teaching tool for each object lesson is provided and, if needed, instructions are outlined.

PRESENTATION: A complete script for an interactive dialogue with the children is offered.

PRAYER: A brief prayer, suitable for repetition by the children, is given as a summary statement of the message.

Although the thirty sermons are listed by title in the contents at the beginning of the book, a significant component of this collection is the Hymn Story Cross-Reference and the Scripture Cross-Reference at the end, along with Teaching Tools and Theological Themes.

Since hymns are the basis for much of the message of our faith and are an integral part of worship, they are a logical place to derive ideas for the children's message. Sermons labeled "Hymn Stories" include suggestions for making or using a teaching tool, a script to be used with the children to convey the story of the hymn, and instructions for leaders so they may prepare for their presentation. Of course, to best connect the lesson with the words of each hymn, an effort should be made to sing the song in worship before the sermon is shared.

Why is this book needed?

This book is a ready-to-use collection of messages to help children explore various aspects of the sacrament of baptism. Although books of children's sermons might include one meditation on this theme— at the most—there is no other resource that puts many explanations of the topic into one book. Since baptism is celebrated many times throughout the year, this collection provides a valuable tool for the variety of occasions that focus on the sacrament. Church leaders can readily find help for lessons, whether ideas are needed to celebrate the actual baptism of infants, children, youth, or adults; to mark events such as blessings, confirmations, and dedications; or to explore the seasons of the church year.

Who will use this book?

This book will be used in congregations by clergy, Christian educators, Sunday school leaders, and laypersons; in parochial schools by administrators and teachers; and in homes by parents and grandparents.

Messages are designed for children in kindergarten through grade five but are adaptable for boys and girls in preschool and young people in middle grades. They will also be appreciated by adults of all ages and appropriate for intergenerational audiences.

How will this book be most helpful?

In congregations, this collection will be used as children's sermons in worship, homilies in children's church, messages in Sunday school classes, reflections in midweek ministries, meditations in youth groups, and devotions at camp. They will also be useful as lessons in confirmation classes and baptism-education programs. In Christian schools, they will be used in chapel services and classroom talks. In families, they will be helpful as a focus for mealtime devotions, faith formation, and bedtime stories.

1
Accepted by God: Cornelius's Baptism

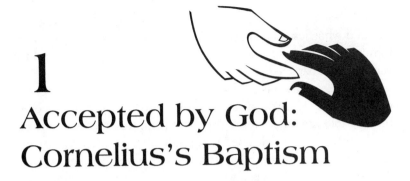

PASSAGE: Acts 10:1–48

PURPOSE: Baptism is available to all who accept God's offer of forgiveness and who believe in Jesus as their Savior from sin.

PREPARATION: People from the congregation of different ages and ethnic backgrounds: infant, child, youth, and adult.

PRESENTATION:
(Invite people from the congregation of different ages and ethnic backgrounds to come forward. Include an infant, child, youth, and adult.) I've invited several people from our congregation to join us this morning. When you look at all of these people, what do you think that they have in common? *(Respond to answers from the children.)* Those are good ideas, but I was thinking that all of these people can be baptized and become part of the church. You may not think that is such a big deal, but there was a time when it was a very big deal. The apostle Peter thought that Jesus came to save only Jewish people. He wouldn't even think of baptizing someone who wasn't Jewish. Then God sent Peter a vision that changed all that.

Peter saw a sheet full of all kinds of animals being lowered from heaven. It was filled with animals that God had told the Jewish people were unclean and could not be eaten. Then Peter heard God say, "Eat." Peter said, "Lord, I can't eat these, they are unclean." God said to him, "Don't call unclean what I tell you is clean." Just then the servant of a Roman soldier named Cornelius came looking for Peter. The soldier had been sent to get Peter so Cornelius could hear about Jesus. Peter went to see Cornelius and told him the gospel message—the good news of salvation. When Cornelius heard who Jesus was and what Jesus had done, he and everyone who was there with him believed and wanted to become part of God's family. And they wanted to be baptized.

Before seeing the vision, Peter would not even have spoken to Cornelius because Cornelius wasn't a Jew. Now Peter not only spoke to him, he told him about Jesus' life, death, and resurrection. Peter baptized Cornelius and welcomed him into the family of God. Ever since then, the church has been baptizing everyone who believes in Jesus. It doesn't make any difference who they are, or how old they are, or what color their skin is, or whether they are a man or a woman. All who believe in Jesus can be baptized and welcomed into God's family.

PRAYER:
Dear God, thank you for accepting us into the family of faith—just as we are. Amen.

2
Called to Repentance: Jordan's Significance

PASSAGE: Matthew 3:1–6

PURPOSE: Baptism is an ancient rite that symbolizes repentance, a promise before God that one intends to change.

PREPARATION: Map of Israel

PRESENTATION:

(Hold up the map of Israel.) Have you ever looked at a map of the Holy Land? What important places do you recognize on it? *(Some may name or point to places like Bethlehem, Jericho, Jerusalem, or Nazareth.)* What about this river? *(Point to the Jordan River.)* Do you suppose this river might be important since much of this land is dry like a desert? Yes, indeed! This is the Jordan River, and it was a significant source of life and water for the people of Israel in Bible times—and still is today. The Jordan River is about seventy miles long, stretching between the Sea of Galilee and the Dead Sea. It was beside the Jordan River that the Israelites renewed their covenant with God before entering the promised land with Joshua.

Have you ever heard of a man named John the Baptist? *(Invite responses and guide explanations.)* Yes, he's the son who was born to Elizabeth and Zechariah just a little while before Jesus was born to Mary and Joseph. He was really Jesus' cousin. And it was John who challenged Israel to renew their covenant with God. He preached along the banks of the Jordan River and baptized those who heard the message to "Repent and be saved!" John also baptized Jesus in the Jordan River.

Even today some people travel to Israel in order to be baptized or rebaptized in the waters of the Jordan. Sometimes people bring home containers of Jordan River water to be placed in baptismal fonts here so that they feel connected to that special river where Jesus was baptized by John.

I'm certain that those who make the journey to the Jordan River are blessed by their experience. However, it is not the place on the map where we are baptized that really matters. What place is important at baptism? *(Point to your heart.)* Yes, our hearts are the places where the change must happen. That's what John preached and understood. Baptism symbolizes a change of heart. We turn away from sin and turn toward God. We don't need a map to find a place to do that. We can make our promise to God and use whatever water is at hand. That's all that John asked people to do, and that's what Jesus commanded the disciples to do. Whether we are baptized in a river, in a pond, or in a church, what really matters is that we hear the two-thousand-year-old message to "Repent and be saved!"

PRAYER:

Dear God, thank you for messengers like John who invite people to the water of baptism. Help us to remember our promise to turn from sin and to turn toward you. Amen.

3
Challenged to Remember: Christ's Sacrifice

PASSAGE: Mark 15:1–39

PURPOSE: Baptism is a gift that challenges us to remember the high cost of Christ's sacrifice.

PREPARATION: Bucket of water, sponge

PRESENTATION:
(*Hold up a dry sponge.*) What do I have here? (*A sponge.*) Yes, this is a sponge. What do you notice about this sponge? (*Accept all observations.*) Those are good observations, but the one I wanted you to notice is that this sponge is absolutely dry and hard. What do you think is missing to make this sponge soft and easy to use? (*Water.*) Right! In order to be useful, the sponge needs to be moist. It needs to have water.

Can you remember anything about a sponge in the story of Jesus' Crucifixion? (*Let a volunteer explain.*) Yes, when Jesus was on the cross, one of the bystanders filled a sponge with vinegar and offered him a drink. What a sad feeling we get when we remember the difficulties Jesus faced on the cross. What kinds of challenges do you think Jesus had to deal with? (*Brainstorm ideas like embarrassment, fatigue, loneliness, pain, and thirst.*)

Why would Jesus go through so much suffering? (*See what listeners think.*) Jesus chose to do things God's way, even when it was difficult. Jesus understood that accepting the challenge of the cross would provide the way to be saved for all who believe in him. Jesus accepted God's challenge and gave his life out of love for you and me.

When we are baptized into Christ's death with him, we are challenged to do things God's way too. Following God is not always easy, but accepting God's challenge makes our lives fulfilling. Without the water of baptism we are like this dry sponge—not useful. But once we belong to Christ, dead to our sins and alive to eternal life, then we can be good for something. *(Plunge the dry sponge into a bucket of water.)* We can bounce back from difficulty, and our lives take on new purpose and possibility. *(Squeeze the sponge.)*

We cannot understand all of the challenges Jesus faced in order to bring us the gift of eternal life. However, we can accept the challenge to absorb the life-giving water of baptism so that we can become useful to God. When we are baptized, we are challenged to do things "God's way": to use our lives to bring joy and blessing to others as Christ used his death and resurrection to bring us the gift of salvation.

PRAYER:
Dear God, thank you that Jesus was willing to accept the challenge of death on a cross. Help us to accept the challenges of life, knowing that your love will sustain us. Amen.

4

Changed by God:
Paul's
Conversion

PASSAGE: Acts 9:1–20

PURPOSE: Baptism begins a lifelong process of change, creating disciples who live in the world by the power of the Holy Spirit.

PREPARATION: Ice cube tray, kettle, pitcher

PRESENTATION:
(*Hold up ice cube tray, kettle, and pitcher.*) What do these three things have in common? (*Listen to any suggestions but affirm or propose that they all hold water.*) The water that each of these holds is quite different. What do we expect of water that is in this tray? (*It would be ice.*) And in the pitcher? (*Liquid.*) And from the kettle? (*Point to the spout and suggest steam.*) Ice, liquid, and steam are forms of the same element called water—H_2O.

Some people have used this idea to help Christians understand the Trinity—God as Parent, Son, and Holy Spirit. We talk about God as our creator, Jesus as our savior, and the Holy Spirit as our ever-present unseen power, but we are really talking about only one God. When we are baptized, we are baptized in the name of the Father, the Son, and the Holy Spirit—three ways to understand or experience God but only one God.

Just like water can change, so can people. Not long after Jesus was crucified, a man named Saul—who was very religious—believed that the new faith called Christianity was wrong. He arrested and ordered Christians to be killed. Once when he was on his way to a city called Damascus in order to get rid of more followers of Jesus, a blinding light stopped Saul, and he fell to the ground. The voice of Jesus spoke to Saul and changed his heart completely. Another man, named Annanias, heard God's voice too, telling him to go to pray for Saul to receive his eyesight. Saul's eyes were opened, he received the Holy Spirit, and he was baptized in the name of Jesus. Saul's name was changed to Paul, and he became God's special messenger of faith to all people.

The water of baptism begins a change in us too. Being baptized Christians means that we must let God melt our cold, selfish hearts and change us to more caring, giving people. Then as the fire of the Spirit continues to warm our hearts, our enthusiasm for God's mission increases and we reach out to others, just like steam in the teakettle moves up and out into the air. When we invite God into our lives at baptism, we begin a lifelong process of change. Like Paul, we begin a journey based on faith, trusting in God's Spirit to lead us to take the good news of Jesus Christ to the world.

PRAYER:
Dear God, thank you for giving us many ways to understand you. Help us to change more each day into the loving people we are called to be. Amen.

5
Cherished by God: Abraham's Covenant

PASSAGE: Genesis 17:1–7, 15–16

PURPOSE: Baptism reaffirms the covenant relationship between God and God's cherished children, those who follow in faith as descendants of Abraham.

PREPARATION: Globe or world map

PRESENTATION:
(Hold up globe or map.) Can you help me find all the oceans on the earth? *(Take time to point out and name as many as time permits—Atlantic, Antarctic, Arctic, Indian, and Pacific.)* Wow! There are five major oceans and several smaller seas. But look—it seems to me that they are not really separate bodies of water. It looks like they are all connected. *(With a finger, trace the oceans across the globe or map.)*

The world is more than 70 percent water. No wonder God chose water as a symbol to remind us that we are loved and cherished. Water is all around us, just like God! The water of baptism reminds us that those who believe and are baptized are also connected with one another. We are all one family of God. In baptism we promise to place our trust in God, and God promises to love and care for us and to be with us wherever we go. That covenant, or promise, goes back over four thousand years to a man named Abraham and his wife Sarah in the Hebrew Scriptures.

Abraham was an old man who had no children. But he believed God's promise that he would be the father of many nations, with more descendants than stars in the sky or grains of sand on the shore. Abraham must have had a lot of faith. When Abraham and Sarah were in their nineties, God did give them a son, Isaac, whose descendants became the people of Israel, which also includes Jesus. Because we are Jesus' brothers and sisters in faith, that makes us descendants of Abraham and children of God's promise as well.

Abraham was considered righteous—God's friend—because of his faith. When we are baptized, we choose, like Abraham, to put our faith in God and to live in a covenant relationship. We promise to be faithful to God, and God promises to be faithful to us. Guess who's better at keeping the promise? God is.

We human beings tend to forget our promises. We often sin and fail to live up to our end of the bargain of faithfulness. But God is good. God sent us a savior, Jesus Christ. We know that God cherished Jesus and gave him power over sin and death. Jesus shares freely with us the gift of God's love and grace. Jesus came to let us know that we are God's cherished children too. All of us. Like one great ocean on the earth, we are baptized into one body of believers.

PRAYER:
Dear God, thank you for your promise to love and cherish us always. Help us to remember that your love surrounds us like the ocean. Amen.

6
Claimed by God: Noah's Ark

PASSAGE: Genesis 6:11–9:17

PURPOSE: Baptism symbolizes God's saving power that claims each of us as God's children.

PREPARATION: Baptismal font with water; example of ark

PRESENTATION:

(If possible, sit near the baptismal font.) Have any of you ever seen someone being baptized? What happens? *(Invite a volunteer to explain the procedure.)* Everyone who belongs to Christ experiences the sacrament called baptism. This is our baptismal font. *(Point to the font.)* Who knows what's in it? Yes, water. Baptism uses water to symbolize our connection to God. Actually, the water associated with baptism goes all the way back to a person in the Hebrew Scriptures named Noah. Then water came as a flood that washed away sin from the earth. Why didn't Noah get washed away with the rest of creation? *(Pause for an answer.)* Right, because God saved Noah by helping Noah build an ark. *(Show an example of an ark.)*

Noah was a man who followed God even when nobody else around him chose to accept God's ways. Everyone else ignored God and lived selfishly and sinfully. God saw Noah's faithfulness and chose him to be the one God would use to start the human race over again. God told Noah exactly how to build the boat that could survive the great flood that God knew was coming. The Bible tells us that the boat was big enough to hold two of each kind of animal, as well as Noah, his family, and their supplies. Then it began to rain.

How long did it rain? (*Find a consensus on forty days and forty nights*). Yes, in other words, it rained a long time.

The waters swelled and covered all the earth, but Noah and his family were safe inside the ark. Finally, Noah knew it was safe to take his family off the ark and to begin living on dry ground again. God blessed Noah and promised that the earth would never again be destroyed by water. Then God placed a rainbow in the sky as a sign of that promise, God's covenant with Noah and with us. The church is our ark, and water is our symbol for God's power to save us. The water in our baptismal font symbolizes God's power to save us from sin—just like the ark saved Noah.

I wonder why God would use something as simple and ordinary as water to help us know that we are saved and loved? (*Affirm any respondents.*) Water is really a very important ingredient to life on Earth. Without water we couldn't exist. Everyone—whether rich or poor, strong or weak, young or old—must have water to survive. Water is God's symbol of life to the world. Just as our world must have water to live, those who are baptized understand that we must have God's presence to have eternal life. The baptismal font helps us remember the promise of baptism: We are saved by God's power and claimed as God's children.

PRAYER:
Dear God, thank you for claiming us as your own. Help us to remember that we belong to you. Amen.

7
Cleansed by God: Nicodemus's Lesson

PASSAGE: John 3:1–21

PURPOSE: Baptism uses outer cleansing with water to represent God's inner cleansing and forgiveness.

PREPARATION: Basin and pitcher

PRESENTATION:

How many of you washed your hands yesterday? How many washed your hands today? Wait a minute. Some of you raised your hands both times. If you washed yesterday, why do you need to wash your hands again today? (*Let someone explain about cleanliness and germs.*) Washing is something that must be repeated again and again. In earlier days, before indoor running water, every home had at least one of these: a basin and pitcher. (*Show the illustration.*)

Wherever human beings live, they need water to use for washing. The church also uses water in baptism to help human beings understand the cleansing power of God's love and forgiveness. The water of baptism is simply an outward sign of God's cleansing that really happens on the inside, in our hearts. Jesus once told a man named Nicodemus that becoming part of God's kingdom meant being "born again." Nicodemus was a Pharisee, a religious leader and teacher. Most Pharisees didn't like Jesus, because they were jealous of his power. But Nicodemus was curious about Jesus.

One night Nicodemus went to see Jesus in order to learn more about what Jesus was teaching. Jesus told Nicodemus that everyone could find God's power by being reborn. Nicodemus thought it was silly to imagine being born again from his mother, but Jesus told him about spiritual rebirth, about being changed on the inside by God's Holy Spirit. Apparently Nicodemus learned the difference between cleansing on the outside that doesn't last and cleansing on the inside that means being changed forever by God's power. At Jesus' trial, Nicodemus spoke up when he asked about justice for Jesus and then later worked with Joseph of Arimathea to arrange Jesus' burial. Nicodemus must have learned what it meant to be born again.

Being born again is what baptism represents—that we have been cleansed on the inside and have received the grace of God's acceptance, just as though we were newborn. We have to wash our bodies over and over again, but we don't have to be baptized over and over again. The basin and pitcher remind us of the water we must use every day to keep our bodies clean, but the water we use every day can also remind us of the water we use only once in baptism. The water of baptism outwardly symbolizes the grace of God that remains with us on the inside—forever.

PRAYER:

Dear God, thank you for the water of baptism and for the gift of your grace. Help us to remember every day that we are made new on the inside by the Holy Spirit's power. Amen.

8
Commissioned by Christ: Disciples' Instructions

PASSAGE: Matthew 28:16–20

PURPOSE: Baptism commissions us to share with others the good news that Jesus lives and offers eternal life to those who believe and are baptized in his name.

PREPARATION: Fountain

PRESENTATION:
(If possible display a functioning fountain; use a picture and sound effects if necessary.) Don't the sounds of the fountain seem joyful? The water just bubbles up and overflows. That's a wonderful water symbol for Christian joy. What are some reasons for joy in life? *(Affirm responses or prompt with questions like "Does anyone have any new life to celebrate—a new kitten or puppy, a new baby brother or sister?")* We have many reasons to be joyful, but the greatest reason of all is symbolized in Christian baptism. Baptism celebrates that Jesus rose from the dead and lives and reigns in heaven. Baptism reminds us that death is not the end of life's story. The disciples thought that Jesus' crucifixion ended everything. But Christ rose on the third day after his crucifixion. When Jesus appeared to Mary Magdalene, he told her to go and tell the others that he was alive. Can you imagine how happy they were to learn that God had performed the greatest miracle of all? Wouldn't you have liked to have Mary's job—to share the good news with everyone else that she had seen Jesus? Guess what? You do.

After Mary told the disciples about Jesus' resurrection, Jesus appeared to them too. The Bible reports that Jesus stayed on earth for forty days after the resurrection; then he called the disciples together for their final instructions. Jesus commissioned them—or gave them special authority—that they were to go into all the world to preach, teach, and baptize. Those who were baptized by the first disciples told the next generation, and they told the next, until finally someone shared with us the good news that because Christ lives, we too shall live. Now we have the same duty as Mary and the disciples did, to let others know that Jesus has overcome the power of death. We serve a risen Savior who lives on earth in the hearts of those who are baptized in his name.

A fountain is a wonderful reminder that the joy of Jesus lives deep in our souls, but it does not stay there. The delight we feel as baptized believers must bubble out and overflow to others. We cannot contain it. If we truly live the message of our baptism and the good news of Jesus' resurrection, then we must share the message with others. Those are your orders. You are commissioned to go and tell.

PRAYER:
Dear God, thank you for the good news that Jesus lives. Thank you for commissioning us to let others know our joy of being baptized believers. Amen.

9
Confessed in Faith: Christ's Name

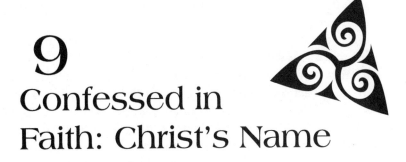

PASSAGE: Philippians 2:9–11

PURPOSE: Baptism is the celebration of God's grace in which we confess faith in Jesus, we are named before God, and we are welcomed into the church in the name of God the Father (Creator), the Son (Redeemer), and the Holy Spirit.

PREPARATION: Triangle

PRESENTATION:

(Hold up a large triangle.) What does a triangle have to do with Christian worship, especially baptism? *(Welcome any suggestions, but guide discussion toward thinking about the meaning of the number three.)* What idea about God do we understand that is explained in the number three? *(The Trinity.)* When someone is baptized, we baptize the person in the name of God the _____. *(See if the participants can complete the phrase for the Trinity.)* Yes, we think of God as father, mother, parent, or creator; as son or savior; and as Holy Spirit or ever-present power. Although we use three names for God, there is only one God, much like this triangle has three sides but is only one shape. That's why the triangle is a symbol in the church—it represents the Trinity, our three ways of knowing God. *(Point out any triangles in the architecture of the building or in the stained glass windows.)*

The names for God that we understand in the Trinity are an important part of baptism. When we are baptized, we are named before God, and we confess the name that is above all names—Jesus. Then the pastor uses water, symbolizing God's cleansing power, to baptize us in the name of God the Father, the Son, and the Holy Spirit.

(Point to the three sides of the triangle.) That means that we are claimed by God who made us in the first place, by Jesus who died in our place to forgive our sin, and by the Holy Spirit who will live within us and guide us all of our days.

Naming is an important part of baptism. When the minister says our name at baptism, we celebrate that as a child of God, God knows us by name. When we say Christ's name, affirming that Jesus is the Lord of our lives, we accept the name of "disciple." When we receive the Holy Spirit, we are made one with other believers and become brothers and sisters in the family of faith. So the person being baptized is named as a child of God, as a disciple of Christ, and as a member of the church. *(Point to the three sides of the triangle again.)* With baptism we are a trinity of meanings too, but we are really only one person with a new name—Christian.

PRAYER:
Dear God, thank you that you know us by name. Help us to remember to call upon your name as we live as Christians in your world. Amen.

10
Confirmed in Faith: Our Promise

HYMN STORY: "O Jesus, I Have Promised"

PASSAGE: Ephesians 1:13–14

PURPOSE: At confirmation we affirm our baptismal response to God's love and we promise, with the help of the Holy Spirit, to follow and to serve Jesus.

PREPARATION: Materials to make a sealed note: crosses (metal, plastic, or wood), envelope, foil, glue, matches, newspaper, pen, sealing wax or candles, spools, stationery or paper, three sheets per project. Access to the hymn "O Jesus, I Have Promised." Invite the congregation to sing the hymn before sharing the children's sermon.

METHOD:

Prepare a sealed note to use as the sample illustration for the story of the hymn "O Jesus, I Have Promised." Fold three sheets of paper or stationery into thirds. On one piece leave the inside blank, but write "Jesus" in the center of the outside. Fold up the sheet. On the second paper write, "Dear Children, I have written a hymn containing all the important truths I want you to remember when you are fully confirmed." Place the date "1868" in the upper right hand corner and sign the note with the name "John Ernest Bode." Fold this letter around the first note. On the third message write, "Dear Friends, follow me," on the inside, and address it to the "Believers at (*Name of congregation*)." Fold the third letter around the other two notes.

Seal the parcel with the stamp of a cross. Construct the stamp by gluing a three-dimensional metal, plastic, or wood cross shape to one end of a spool. The spool serves as the handle for the stamp. Use commercial sealing wax or candle drippings for the project. If candle drippings are used, the wax must be very hot. Cover the work surface with newspaper. Light the candle, and carefully drip wax onto a piece of foil. Dip the stamp into the hot wax, and immediately press the cross shape onto the letter sealing the open edges together.

PRESENTATION:

Have you ever received a note that had a seal on the back like this? *(Hold up sealed note.)* Probably not. But long ago, before envelopes had glue on them, people sealed notes with wax and their own special designs so that the person who was to read the message knew that no one else had broken the seal and read the contents. The special design of the stamp, the tool used to mark the sealing wax, let the receiver of the note know the identity of the person who had sent it. The stamp and seal was sort of a promise that the message was real and to be believed. We still "seal" and "stamp" our letters today—but in a different way. This note is stamped with a cross. Shall we break the seal and see what the note says? It seems to be addressed to us—"Believers at *(Name of congregation)*." *(Open seal.)*

The note reads: "Dear Friends, follow me," and it is signed, "Jesus." And here's another note inside. This one is already open. It is dated 1868 and is signed by a man named John Ernest Bode, an Anglican minister, and is written to his three children, a daughter and two sons who were all to be confirmed on the same day. It reads, "Dear Children, I have written a hymn containing all the important truths I want you to remember when you are fully confirmed."

Well, I have to admit that I made these notes, but the words in them are real. Jesus really does ask those who believe to follow him. And a man named John Ernest Bode really did write a hymn called "O Jesus, I Have Promised" for his three children on their confirmation day. Confirmation is the special service for youth to confirm, or seal, the promises their parents made for them at baptism. They make the promise their own—a promise to follow Jesus and a promise to serve others. Here is another note. This one is addressed to Jesus, but right now it is blank. You see, each of us must respond to Jesus' invitation to follow. What John Bode taught his children in the hymn is that believers can say "yes" to Jesus because Jesus himself will stay near to help us keep the promise.

So we have three notes representing three parts to a very important promise. The first part of the promise comes from God at baptism, when God makes us God's own and promises to be our God. The second part of the promise comes from those who bring us to God, most often our parents, that they will raise us to know God and teach us the way of faith. The final promise—the one John Bode's hymn is about—is our response to God's love. Each one of us must make the promise for himself or herself. We promise that we will follow and serve Jesus wherever he leads—but we have the assurance that Jesus goes with us to guide us, shield us, and befriend us. That seems like a pretty good arrangement—one worth setting our seal to.

Let's make our promise: "Jesus, I promise to serve thee to the end." *(Write the words on the paper.)* And let's mark it with our seal. The message is real, and we claim it as our own. *(Complete the sealing of the envelope as a group or individual project as appropriate.)*

PRAYER:
Dear God, thank you for the invitation to follow and to serve. Help us to keep our promise and to live our vows by sealing us with your Holy Spirit. Amen.

11

Connected to God: Christ's Resurrection

PASSAGE: Colossians 2:12

PURPOSE: The act of baptism connects believers to God by symbolically burying them with Christ and raising them to new life.

PREPARATION: Hose

PRESENTATION:

Who knows what I have here? A garden hose. Right! What is a garden hose used for? (*Brainstorm a list.*) Yes, a garden hose can help fill anything from sprinkling cans to swimming pools. It is also useful to bring water to plants in a garden or flowers in a yard to keep them alive when it doesn't rain. Every gardener needs a garden hose. But suppose that this hose wasn't connected to anything. Then would it be helpful? No! Without being connected to a source of water, the hose cannot fill anything or bring life to any plant.

The water of baptism comes to Christians in many ways, usually not in a garden hose but in a special container like a baptistery or a baptismal font. Some Christians are simply sprinkled with water in their baptism, others are immersed in special pools or in rivers or lakes. But no matter how a Christian is baptized, what is important is that those who share the water of baptism are connected to the source of life, to God in Jesus Christ. Baptism is a drama that reenacts the story of Christ's triumph over death. Jesus submitted to death on the cross, was placed in the tomb, and was resurrected to eternal life.

When we experience the water over our heads, we are symbolically being buried with Christ. We accept his sacrifice for our sins. His death becomes ours. When we rise up from baptism, we are raised to new life, just as Christ overcame death through his resurrection. When we submit to baptism, we act out the truth that we are dead to sin and alive in the Holy Spirit.

When we fully understand what baptism means, then we know that we are connected to the source of God's love and power. Being connected to God means that God's Holy Spirit will flow through us, just as water flows through this garden hose when it is connected. Now every time you use the hose to water plants or to fill the wading pool, you can remember that through your baptism you are connected to Jesus Christ, the source of eternal life.

PRAYER:
Dear God, thank you for giving us the water of baptism to remind us that we are brought from death to life. Keep us connected to Christ, our source of eternal life. Amen.

12
Covered by Grace: Water's Message

PASSAGE: Acts 8:26–40

PURPOSE: Baptism takes place through many methods, but water is the unifying symbol, connecting all who believe with Christ.

PREPARATION: Containers filled with water such as basin, bottle, bowl, bucket, pitcher, sprayer, or vase.

PRESENTATION:
(Show a variety of containers that hold water.) What do all of these containers have in common? *(Encourage guesses, but build to the consensus that they all contain water.)* These containers can help us understand something important about baptism. All churches use water to symbolize God's power to cleanse us and to change our hearts. But not all churches use water in the same way. Some have deep baptismal pools, or they use nearby lakes or rivers where they immerse their members. In these churches, believers who want to be baptized might put on special white robes and wade into water about waist high. There the pastor helps the person make a commitment to Christ and then dips the new believer into the water—sometimes leaning them backwards, sometimes forwards—until they are completely covered by the water, maybe as many as three times. Other churches use basins or fonts of water from which they sprinkle, pour, or anoint believers with the sign of the cross. In these traditions, the pastor takes water and places it on the head of the child or adult seeking baptism. Although the methods of baptism might be different, the symbol of the water and

of the water's meaning remains the same—the washing away of our sins in the name of Jesus Christ.

One story in the Bible that helps us understand that water is the important symbol for those who want to accept the good news of Jesus' death and resurrection is about an Ethiopian official and the apostle Philip. In the story told in Acts 8, Philip was led by the Holy Spirit to find the Ethiopian who was seeking God with his whole heart. Philip explained a passage from the book of Isaiah that the man had trouble understanding, a passage that foretold the death of Jesus. When the Ethiopian understood that Jesus came to earth to bring God's forgiving love, he wanted Philip to baptize him then and there. "Here's water!" he exclaimed. They stopped their chariot right on the spot, and Philip baptized the eager new believer with the water that was at hand. What was important was not the method of his baptism—anointing, immersion, pouring, or sprinkling—but that the water symbolized the washing away of his sin and his acceptance into the Christian faith.

Water takes the shape of whatever container it fills, whether that shape is a bowl or a bottle, a lake or a baptismal font. The water, however, holds the same cleansing power for all those who open their hearts to God. Although the water may go on our heads or over our entire bodies, what we are saying is, "God create in me a clean heart and make me one with Christ." Then we become the container for God's Holy Spirit as we live lives that show God's love to others.

PRAYER:
Dear God, thank you for the many forms that water may take. Help us to remember that water symbolizes your forgiveness and acceptance of us in Jesus' name. Amen.

13
Dedicated to God: Love's Response

PASSAGE: Luke 2:25–40

PURPOSE: Dedication is the holy act of setting apart as sacred the life of one who is given to God.

PREPARATION: Anointing oil

PRESENTATION:

All people who become Christians are baptized, but not all Christians are baptized at the same age. In some churches or in some families baptism is reserved for children or adults who are old enough to choose the sacrament for themselves. Often in those congregations babies are dedicated, not baptized. To dedicate someone is to set the person apart for a special purpose or to establish a special relationship with God.

When Jesus was eight days old, Mary and Joseph took him to the temple in Jerusalem to be dedicated. In fact there were two dedicated people waiting at the temple, hoping to see God's Chosen One. One of these people was Simeon, an old man who God had promised would live to see the Messiah. Another special person was Anna, an old woman who had prayed and fasted in the temple day and night for a long, long time. She too hoped to see God's gift of a savior. Because of their dedication both of these people were in place, ready to recognize God's gift in Jesus. They worshiped God with thanksgiving and told Jesus' parents how special their child would become. That must have been a memorable moment for Mary and Joseph.

Today a service that symbolizes a child's special relationship with God is called a dedication. Sometimes in a dedication, children are anointed. *(Hold up a container of anointing oil. If appropriate, allow the participants to place a bit of oil on their fingers.)* In the Bible, oil was used to set people apart for a special purpose. In the Hebrew Scriptures prophets anointed kings, and in the Christian Scriptures, a woman anointed Jesus. In a dedication today, anointing oil can be used to mark those we want to bless and offer to God's care and protection.

Does the mark remain visible for all to see? No. Soon there is no way to tell that someone has been anointed or dedicated. But we can see people's actions. Those who live their lives for God show their dedication by their choices like Simeon and Anna showed their dedication by their actions in the temple. Parents who dedicate their children promise that they will train them in God's ways and model Jesus' love in their own family.

That's what it means to be dedicated—to do the things that we promise. When we make a holy promise to God, the oil of anointing may disappear, but God's love in our lives is visible for everyone to see.

PRAYER:
Dear God, thank you for people in our lives who are dedicated to serving you. Help us to live so that other people may see that we are dedicated to you, too. Amen.

14

Empowered for Ministry: Jesus' Baptism

HYMN STORY: "When Jesus Came to Jordan"

PASSAGE: Matthew 3:13–17

PURPOSE: Baptism is God's granting of approval and blessing, symbolized by the descending dove.

PREPARATION: Dove symbol. Have access to the hymn "When Jesus Came to Jordan." Invite the congregation to sing the hymn before sharing the children's sermon.

PRESENTATION:

Did you know that Jesus was baptized? When do you think Jesus received his baptism? Was it (A) When he was a baby in Bethlehem? (B) When he was at the temple at age twelve? (C) When he was a grown man ready to begin his ministry? Or is the answer really (D) Jesus wasn't baptized because he never sinned. How many think it was D? A? B? How many think C? Congratulations! C is correct. Jesus was baptized in the Jordan River by his cousin John when he was about thirty years old. But we believe that Jesus was without sin, so why did he have to be "cleansed" in baptism?

In the Bible story John tells Jesus that he is not worthy to baptize him, but Jesus insists. Jesus says that they should fulfill God's plan for his life. At baptism Jesus gave himself to God, accepting everything that God wanted him to do, including dying for the forgiveness of our sin. When Jesus accepted his mission from God the Bible says the "heavens opened," and Jesus saw the Holy Spirit of God descending like a dove. *(Show the dove symbol.)* God spoke, proclaiming, "This is my beloved son." Those who heard the message knew that Jesus was the promised Messiah, the ruler who would save God's people.

That's an important story to tell, don't you think? It helps us understand the meaning of our baptism. That is what a man named Fred Pratt Green believed too. A friend of his was concerned when he thought a new Australian hymnal wouldn't have any songs to celebrate the story of the baptism of Jesus. So in 1973 Fred agreed to write the words for a hymn that recorded the events of Jesus' baptism. Today Christians around the world sing his song, "When Jesus Came to Jordan."

The last line of the hymn reminds us of the important symbol of the descending dove. The words tell us that Jesus was baptized—not because he needed to be forgiven—but because we needed to know that he was God's Son, sent to bring us forgiveness. When we are baptized, we celebrate that we are forgiven because we need God's cleansing. However, we also remember that, like Jesus, we too need God's Holy Spirit to come into our lives to lead us to the mission God has for us.

PRAYER:
Dear God, thank you for the story of Jesus' baptism. Help us to sense the presence of your Holy Spirit in our lives. Amen.

15
Filled with the Spirit: Pentecost's Power

Passage: Acts 2:37–42

Purpose: Baptism is the believer's response to understanding that Jesus died to bring us forgiveness and new life.

Preparation: Candle, matches

Presentation:

I have one of the symbols of Pentecost in my hand. *(Hold up an unlit candle.)* Well, actually, I don't. This candle is missing the Pentecost symbol. Can you guess what's missing? Yes! The flame. *(Light the candle.)* Flames symbolize the message of Pentecost because in the second chapter of the book of Acts, where the first Pentecost is described, the Bible says that the disciples seemed to have tongues of flames resting on each one of them. That must have made quite a picture. When John baptized Jesus in the Jordan River, John claimed that Jesus would baptize his followers with fire. Fire represents the energy and enthusiasm that comes to those who open their lives completely to God's indwelling presence.

On the first Pentecost Peter preached a sermon to the people in the marketplace at Jerusalem. He told them how Jesus came to die for their sins, and he explained that although they had crucified Jesus, he was not dead. Peter proclaimed Jesus' resurrection for the first time in public. And the people were amazed at God's power. They suddenly understood how much God loved them and how much Jesus went through to offer them the hope of life after death. When people come to understand God's love and Jesus' sacrifice, they want to do something in response. So the people in the crowd asked Peter, "What can we do?" Do you know what Peter told them? He gave them the first two steps in becoming a Christian: repent and be baptized. To repent means that you are truly sorry for your sins, and to be baptized means that you open your heart to God's love and forgiveness.

The water of baptism symbolizes our spiritual cleansing and the beginning of a new life in Christ. Sometimes at baptism we burn a special candle, even taking it home to light each year on the anniversary of our baptism. The flame of that candle reminds us that we must respond with energy and enthusiasm to the message that Jesus gave his life for us and sends the Holy Spirit to dwell within us. We are like the unlit candle; God provides the fire of the Spirit for our lives.

Because Peter preached the first sermon on Pentecost Day, some folks say that Pentecost is the birthday of the church. That's another good reason to light our candle. Have you ever noticed that one candle can light another without losing any of its own light? That's the way it is with God's love. In baptism we receive God's presence and power for life, and we share that message with others, just like those first listeners to Peter's sermon. After they were baptized, they began to study, to fellowship, to commune, and to pray together. They passed their light on to others who passed it on again until finally today we're here sharing the flame of God's love with one another.

PRAYER:
Dear God, thank you for the warmth and light of your love. Help us to keep the flame of your Holy Spirit in our hearts and use us to help spark the faith of others. Amen.

16
Focused for Mission: Epiphany's Promise

HYMN STORY: "Lord, When You Came to Jordan"

PASSAGE: John 1:29–34

PURPOSE: Baptism is both a revelation of Jesus as the Savior of the world and a revelation that believers share in Christ's mission.

PREPARATION: Star. Access to hymn "Lord, When You Came to Jordan." Invite the congregation to sing the hymn before sharing the children's sermon.

PRESENTATION:

Do any of you celebrate Epiphany? Epiphany is a special day in the church year that occurs on January 6; however, many churches continue the season of Epiphany until the beginning of Lent. What does this shape have to do with Epiphany? (*Show the star.*) I'll give you a hint: Epiphany is the time in the church when we remember the arrival of the wise men at Bethlehem. Now you probably understand that the star represents the message of Epiphany: the wise men followed the heavenly light to find the Christ Child. So Epiphany represents God's light coming into our lives. (*If possible, light the star if it is electrical.*) Ah! Epiphany also means "awakening" or "revelation." Maybe you've seen cartoons where the character gets a light bulb over his head. Aha! It is a moment of understanding. The wise men coming to Jesus is an "aha!" God sent Jesus for the whole world, not just the people of Israel. And Jesus is more than just a baby born in a manger; he is God's Messiah, the chosen one, who came to lead us from darkness to light.

The Sunday after Epiphany brings another special tradition too. We read the story of Jesus' baptism. Do you remember what happens? Jesus comes to John to be baptized in the Jordan River. At first, John refuses because God has told him how special Jesus is. But Jesus convinces John to perform his baptism. Then John witnesses the heavenly dove descend on Jesus, marking him as God's Son. Aha! Jesus is revealed as God's chosen one at his baptism. An Epiphany!

It may seem strange to celebrate Jesus' baptism so soon after Christmas. However, Epiphany helps us understand that Jesus was born to be the Savior of the world, just as his baptism revealed that God had chosen him for this special purpose. In the recently written hymn "Lord, When You Came to Jordan" by English minister Brian Wren, the words remind us that Jesus' baptism is a revelation of his life and mission. The last line of Wren's hymn is a prayer for us to have an Epiphany of our own. Baptism should reveal to us that Jesus is our Savior and that we are called to share this message with the world.

PRAYER:
Dear God, thank you for sending Jesus to the world. Help us to share with others the message that Jesus came to show us the light. Amen.

17
Gifted for Life: Baptism's Remembrance

PASSAGE: John 14:13–14

PURPOSE: Baptism is a source of joy and celebration as we remember Christ's gift of eternal life.

PREPARATION: Anniversary of baptism card or postcard

PRESENTATION:

How many of you have ever received a birthday card? Wow! Everyone? That's really great. It's nice to be remembered on our birthdays, isn't it? Our birthdays are the celebrations of the special moments when life on earth began for us. That is important—and fun! But how many of you have ever gotten a re-birthday card? Your re-birthday is the day on which you were baptized. There are special cards to celebrate the anniversary of a baptism. I brought one to show you. (*Hold up an example of an anniversary of baptism card or postcard.*)

Why would we celebrate the date of our baptism? (*Accept and discuss reasons.*) Well, if your birthday celebrates the day you were born, what would your re-birthday celebrate? The day you were reborn!

The water of baptism symbolizes new birth. We are given Christ's gift of living water, the power of eternal life. Our earthly bodies that are born will not live forever, but when our spirits are made alive in Christ, we receive the same power of the Holy Spirit that raised Jesus from the dead. Because Jesus lives, we too shall live—forever! Wow! That is really worth celebrating, right?

Do you know the date of your baptism? What about your mom's or dad's, brother's, or sister's? Maybe everyone in your family should find out his or her baptismal date so that you can celebrate the gift of living water that Christ gave to each of you. If we remember to celebrate our baptismal dates, then we can remember that even though our bodies may age, we are forever filled with the energy of new life. Then we really will bubble over with joy—we will not only have the days of our life, but we'll have life for our days!

PRAYER:
Dear God, thank you for Christ's gift of living water. Fill us with joy as we remember our baptism. Amen.

18
Guided in Life: Christ's Flock

HYMN STORY: "Savior, Like a Shepherd Lead Us"

PASSAGE: John 10:14–15

PURPOSE: Baptism affirms that we are known to God because God made us and we are precious to God because Jesus "bought us."

PREPARATION: Picture of Jesus the Good Shepherd. Access to hymn "Savior, Like a Shepherd Lead Us." Invite the congregation to sing the hymn before sharing the children's sermon.

PRESENTATION:

When we are baptized into the church, we become part of a "flock." In the Bible, Jesus called himself the "Good Shepherd." That makes us God's "sheep." (Hold up a picture of Jesus the Good Shepherd.) One of the most famous hymns often sung at a baptism is "Savior, Like a Shepherd Lead Us." The words tell us that we depend on Jesus like sheep depend on a shepherd. The words also remind us that we belong to Jesus because he "bought us" with his own life. This hymn is a meaningful baptismal prayer.

Amazingly, no one knows for sure who wrote this beautiful hymn. Many people believe that the author was a little lady by the name of Dorothy Ann Thrupp, a minister's daughter who wrote children's hymns in the early 1800s in England. Although she wrote many poems, she seldom signed her name to any of her works. So we really can't be sure exactly who wrote "Savior, Like a Shepherd Lead Us," but Dorothy Thrupp seems a very likely choice. If Dorothy Thrupp were here, she could tell us if these words were hers. Human beings recognize what they create. Do you think the same is true for God? You are created by God. Doesn't that mean that God would know you because God made you? Yes, God knows each one of you, just like a shepherd knows his sheep or a poet knows her words.

The man who wrote the music for this hymn was William Bradbury. He was a church musician who composed many popular hymn tunes in his day. He compiled an entire book of hymns to be used in Sunday school because he believed that "good singing" was an important part of a successful program. It took both our anonymous poet and our famous musician to create this beautiful hymn, didn't it? Just like it took both of them to give us this hymn, it takes both God the Creator and Jesus the Savior to give us an understanding of our baptism.

Jesus is our Good Shepherd. He leads us in life, just like a shepherd guides his sheep. But even more important than leading us, Jesus also laid down his life for us and paid the price for our sins. At baptism when we sing the hymn "Savior, Like a Shepherd Lead Us," we remember that we are God's sheep and God recognizes us. We also remember that we are guided by our Good Shepherd, Jesus, whose loving sacrifice means that we belong to God twice: once because God made us and again because Jesus "bought us."

PRAYER:
Dear God, thank you for making us one of your flock. Help us to follow our Good Shepherd who leads us every day of our lives. Amen.

19
Nurtured in Faith: Infant Baptism

PASSAGE: Genesis 17:7; Psalm 22:9–10; Matthew 19:14

PURPOSE: Baptism is a promise by parents that they intend to nurture their child in the Christian faith.

PREPARATION: Baby bottle

PRESENTATION:

Can anyone tell me what this is? (*Hold up a baby bottle.*) That's right, it's a baby bottle. Who can tell me what we use it for? That's right, it is used to feed a baby. People are very excited when a baby is born and becomes part of a family. New parents and grandparents take pictures. Friends often bring presents. But once all the excitement is over we don't just put the baby in a room, shut the door, and forget about him or her, do we? No, we feed it, change it, cuddle it, talk to it, take it to the doctor for checkups, and do all the other things the baby needs to grow physically and emotionally.

God works like that too. God promises to be God to us and to our children. Because of God's promise, many people have their baby baptized to indicate that he or she is a part of God's family. They are saying that they believe Jesus when he said, "Let the little children come to me, and do not stop them; for it is to such as these that the kingdom of heaven belongs" (Matthew 19:14). The parents promise to teach the baby about Jesus and all the things God has done for us. When they tell their children stories from the Bible, it is like they are feeding them with food from God. This spiritual food will help a child grow up to know and love Jesus. David, the king of Israel, must have had parents like that. In Psalm 22:10 he said to God, "Since my mother bore me you have been my God."

When babies are baptized, not only do parents promise to teach them about Jesus, but congregations do too. In many churches the people of the congregation promise to help the child to learn about Jesus. They promise to help the parents raise their child. That is because the baby is now part of a bigger family than just a mother and father and brothers and sisters. When we are baptized we become part of the family of God. We are all brothers and sisters in God's family, and we all have to share the spiritual food that helps us to know Jesus better.

PRAYER:
Dear God, thank you for parents who promise to nurture their child's faith in you and in Jesus, their Savior. Amen.

20
Promised in Faith: God's Covenant

Hymn Story: "Wash, O God, Our Sons and Daughters"

Passage: Jeremiah 31:31–34; Hebrews 8:10–12

Purpose: Baptism transforms all those who seek God's grace by connecting those baptized, their sponsors, and their church community with God.

Preparation: Materials to make a three-piece puzzle: cardboard, foam core, or poster board; pattern for circle; (optional) permanent marker, exacto knife, or scissors. Access to hymn "Wash, O God, Our Sons and Daughters." Invite the congregation to sing the hymn before sharing the children's sermon.

Method:

Cut the shape of a large circle from cardboard, foam core, or poster board. Then cut the circle into three puzzle pieces. Print words on the front and back of each piece. On piece number one, print "Covenant" on one side and "God" on the other side. On piece number two, print "Questions" on one side and "Believer" on the opposite side. On piece number three, print "Answers" on the front side and "Witness" on the back portion.

PRESENTATION:

Let's see if we can connect these puzzle pieces so that we form one circle from the three shapes. *(If possible, allow the participants to match the pieces so that they create a circle.)* Good! You easily put the puzzle together. Did you notice the words written on each side of the puzzle pieces? Let's read the word on each side of our circle. *(Read "Covenant," "Questions," and "Answers." Then turn the circle over and read "God," "Believer," and "Witness.")* These words help us understand some of the puzzling traditions that we experience at baptism.

When someone is baptized, the pastor asks questions, right? *(Hold up the "Questions" side of the puzzle piece.)* Those questions are directed toward the believer who is either the person being baptized or the parent or sponsor bringing an infant or child to be baptized. *(Hold up the "Believer" puzzle piece.)* Those people being questioned about their faith must provide answers, right? *(Hold up the "Answers" side of the puzzle piece.)* And as they give answers that testify to their beliefs, someone must witness their response, someone like the church community. *(Turn the "Witness" puzzle piece over.)* Finally, their questions and answers are made before God. *(Hold up the "God" side of the puzzle piece.)* And God has made a covenant to be our God if we will be God's people. *(Turn the "Covenant" puzzle piece over.)* At baptism we accept God's covenant or promise and make promises of our own.

A covenant is almost like a contract between and among God and God's people that we belong to God and to each other. Baptism seals that contract. A contemporary hymn, "Wash, O God, Our Sons and Daughters" by Ruth Duck, celebrates the covenant of baptism and reminds us of the relationship among baptized believers, their witnesses, and God. The first verse is a prayer for the child of God being baptized, that he or she will be blessed, and washed, and filled with the Holy Spirit. The second verse prays for nurture and guidance for those who witness the baptism: the parents, sponsors, and members of the congregation. The third and final stanza praises God's transforming and re-creating power that is promised to those who enter the covenant of baptism.

The three parts to our puzzle, the three parties of the covenant, and the three verses in Ruth Duck's hymn remind us that when we become part of the family of faith, we are baptized in the name of the Father, the Son, and the Holy Spirit—the God who creates us, our Savior who redeems us, and the Spirit who guides us. Maybe it's not so puzzling after all—at least not when we put all the pieces together.

PRAYER:

Dear God, thank you for your promise to always be our God. Help us to remember that we have promised to be your people. Amen.

21
Purchased with Love: Simon's Mistake

PASSAGE: Acts 8:4–25

PURPOSE: Baptism is the free gift of God's grace that comes to believers who seek God with all their hearts.

PREPARATION: "Magic coin" and paper grocery bag

PRESENTATION:

Do you believe in magic? Some of you say yes, and some say no. Maybe I can convince you to believe in magic with my magic coin! *(Pretend to remove a "coin" from a pocket or purse and "display" it in the palm of the hand.)* Now, you believe in magic, right? Some of you are not convinced? Well, I can prove to you that this is a real magic coin. If I toss it in the air, I can catch the coin in this paper bag, and you will hear it drop. *(Open a paper grocery bag and hold it between the middle finger and the thumb of one hand. With the other hand pretend to "toss" the coin into the air. Pause for a moment, then "catch" the coin by snapping the fingers holding the bag. The thump will imitate the sound of the coin dropping into the bag.)* Now how many of you believe in my magic coin? *(Repeat the trick if necessary.)*

Well, actually, this is only a magic trick. The coin isn't real. *(Demonstrate the secret of the trick.)* We understand, don't we, that magic is always a trick of some kind. We may enjoy and be fascinated by what we don't understand, but in the end we know that there has to be a secret to the illusion. Sadly, some people feel that way about faith. Because they cannot see God, some people think there must be some kind of "trick" when God's people experience God's presence in a special way.

There is a story in the Bible of a man who seemed to think of baptism in that way. His name was Simon the magician. He had amazed the crowds with his magic tricks. Then Philip, one of the disciples, came to town and began to teach the real story of God's power found in Jesus. Simon was baptized along with many in his city. Peter and John then prayed that the people might receive the Holy Spirit, and suddenly those they had prayed for were filled with the Spirit in a powerful way. Simon had observed Peter and John's prayer, but what do you suppose Simon thought he saw? A magic trick! He quickly offered to buy the secret to the trick. He wanted to have this special gift too! Peter scolded Simon for thinking that God's gift of grace was a magic secret that could be bought and sold.

God's gift of grace that we receive at baptism is real. It is more valuable than silver or gold. It cannot be purchased with money because Jesus purchased our forgiveness with his own life. Because of Jesus, God's loving presence and power is freely given to those who seek God with all their hearts. The tricky part is to believe that something that seems too good to be true, God's free gift of forgiveness and love, is genuinely ours—for the asking.

PRAYER:
Dear God, we ask that you fill us with your Holy Spirit's power. We promise to freely share what you give us with all those who need to know about your love. Amen.

22
Received in Faith: Lydia's Welcome

PASSAGE: Acts 16:11–15

PURPOSE: At baptism believers are welcomed into the family of God.

PREPARATION: Welcome mat

PRESENTATION:

Do you know what this is? (*Hold up a welcome mat.*) Some of you may have one at your house. Yes, it's a welcome mat. Many people put them outside their door to say, "Welcome to our home, we're glad you came." Lydia, a woman we read about in the Christian Scriptures, sort of put out a welcome mat for the apostle Paul and his friends. Paul had come to the continent of Europe to tell the people about Jesus. As far as we know, Paul was the first Christian missionary to go to Europe. When he came to a city named Philippi, he found Lydia and some other women down by the river. They were worshiping God, but they didn't know about Jesus. Lydia invited Paul to tell her about Jesus. She welcomed Jesus into her life by believing in him as her Savior. Lydia also welcomed Paul the traveler into her home when she offered him a place to stay. Since Lydia is considered the first person in Europe to believe in Jesus, you could even say that she welcomed Jesus to the continent.

But Lydia wasn't the only one who put out the welcome mat. You could say that Paul also put one out for Lydia and her family. The Bible tells us that Lydia and her household were baptized. When people are baptized, they become part of a new family—God's family. They stand on the welcome mat, the door opens, and God invites them in saying, "Come in; welcome to my family. Now you are one of my children." When Paul baptized Lydia, it was like he was one of God's children sent by God to open the door for a new sister. Lydia's baptism was her welcome into the family of God.

Baptism still welcomes people into God's family. God invites us in and makes us new members of the family of faith. That is why baptism is usually done in front of the congregation, so that we can all welcome our new brother or sister home. Maybe we should put this welcome mat in front of the baptismal font. (*Hold up welcome mat again.*) What do you think?

PRAYER:
Dear God, thank you that Lydia welcomed Paul to the continent of Europe and that she welcomed Jesus into her heart and her home. Help us to follow her example as we let others know that they are welcome to be part of your family, too. Amen.

23
Released from Sin: Jailer's Conversion

PASSAGE: Acts 16:16–35

PURPOSE: God sets those who believe in Jesus, and are baptized into the household of faith, free from the power of sin in their lives.

PREPARATION: Materials to make paper chains: glue, stapler and staples or tape, paper, scissors. Or a plastic chain and saw.

METHOD:

Prepare a paper or a plastic chain that can easily be broken. For a paper chain, cut paper into strips and join each loop by securing it with glue, staples, or tape. If a plastic chain is used, cut through 90 percent of one link so that it will break when it is put under stress.

PRESENTATION:

Do you know what this is? (*Hold up a paper or a plastic chain.*) Yes, it is a chain. It reminds me of a story about the apostle Paul, the great missionary of Christian Scripture times. Paul and his friend Silas were in the city of Philippi telling people about Jesus. This made some folks very angry. They had Paul and Silas arrested, beaten, and thrown in jail. Paul and Silas were even chained so they couldn't escape from their cell. Late that night, while Paul and Silas were praying and singing songs to God, there was a big earthquake. The earthquake opened the doors to the prison and broke their chains. Suddenly they were free to leave, but they stayed right there.

When the jailer saw the doors open, he thought that everyone had run away. He was afraid that he and his family would be punished for losing the prisoners, so he was going to kill himself to save his family from suffering. Paul stopped the jailer from hurting himself and said, "We are all still here." The jailer was surprised that anyone would stay after being set free, but Paul and Silas had stayed so the jailer would not be punished. The jailer was so amazed by their love for him that he knew what they were saying about Jesus' love must be true. Because of Paul and Silas, the jailer believed in Jesus and was baptized along with his entire household. Then the jailer invited Paul and Silas to join with his family in a big celebration.

Not only were Paul and Silas set free from prison that night, but the jailer was also set free from the chains that held him in sin. When the Philippian jailer believed and was baptized God set him free from the chains of sin. (Break chain apart.) And that is exactly what God does for all of us who believe in Jesus and are baptized. Jesus sets us free, makes us part of God's family—the household of faith, and gives us a new life. That really is reason to celebrate, isn't it?

PRAYER:
Dear God, thank you for setting us free from the power of sin in our lives. Help us to celebrate your love for us every day. Amen.

24
Saved by Grace: Moses' Deliverance

PASSAGE: Exodus 14:21–22

PURPOSE: Baptism celebrates our passage from the slavery of sin to the freedom of God's grace.

PREPARATION: Materials to make posters of methods of water transportation: catalogs, magazines or newspapers, glue, markers, poster board, scissors

---

METHOD:

Prepare a poster containing illustrations of various methods of water transportation. Find pictures in catalogs, magazines, or newspapers, such as a canoe, paddleboat, raft, speedboat, wading boots, and water skis. Cut out the photos and glue them to a piece of poster board.

PRESENTATION:

(Hold up a poster of methods of water transportation.) If you had to get across the sea in a hurry, which one of these would you use? *(Discuss which method would be the fastest, the safest, or the most fun.)* What if the only way to cross the sea was your own two feet? Would that present a problem? That would require a miracle, right?

There is a story in the Bible that tells of a miraculous crossing of the sea—the Red Sea to be exact. The story is about Moses and the people of Israel. Moses—with God's help—had finally convinced the Pharaoh to let the nation of Israel return to their homeland. But as Moses led the people away from Egypt, Pharaoh changed his mind and sent his armies in pursuit of his escaping slaves. Suddenly Moses and the people found themselves trapped between the water of the Red Sea and the chariots of Pharaoh's army.

They had no boats, no water skis, no wading boots *(point to whatever pictures are on the poster)*, and no hope. Well, actually, they had more than hope; they had God. Do you know what happened? *(Allow a participant to tell the story.)* Yes, God sent a strong wind that divided the water and made dry ground for the Israelites to cross over from slavery to freedom. They simply passed through the waters.

This famous story from Exodus becomes a symbol for us of baptism. Just like the Israelites passed through the water from slavery to freedom, when we "pass through" the water of baptism, we leave behind our slavery to sin and cross over to freedom through God's grace. And just like the Israelites, we find that passing through the waters brings us to a new place where we can live in peace and freedom.

The story of the Red Sea teaches us that God has always been in the business of providing a way of escape for those who are willing to follow God's plan. But first we have to recognize that we have no way to save ourselves. *(Use a marker to draw an "X" through all the modes of transportation on the poster.)* Baptism is the way we say, "God, we're relying on you to see us through," both in this life and in the promised land of eternal life.

PRAYER:
Dear God, thank you for the stories that show us your plan for our salvation. Help us to trust you to lead us all the way to the promised land of heaven. Amen.

25
Sealed in Baptism: Scripture's Instructions

HYMN STORY: "Baptized in Water"

PASSAGE: John 3:5; Ephesians 1:13

PURPOSE: Baptism is a sacrament of the church commanded by Jesus and taught in the scriptures.

PREPARATION: Bible. Access to hymn "Baptized in Water." Invite the congregation to sing the hymn before sharing the children's sermon.

PRESENTATION:

Have you ever wondered why the entry to church membership is through a sacrament called baptism? It's because of the instruction book! *(Hold up a Bible.)* The Christian Scriptures in the Bible is a manual for what the Christian church should know and do. Not only did the Gospel of Jesus instruct disciples to "preach, teach, and baptize," the other books of the Christian Scriptures continue to explain the importance of baptism and the symbolism of dying with Christ and being raised to new life.

One rather recent hymn, first published in the early 1980s, is called "Baptized in Water," sung to the tune of the song "Morning Has Broken." An English minister, Michael Saward, of Saint Paul's Cathedral in London, wrote the words, using scripture to frame the ideas of each verse of the hymn. Stanza one is based on Titus 3:5–7 and Hebrews 10:14. *(If time permits, have volunteers read the passages aloud.)* The message from those scripture passages is that baptism is for people who believe that Jesus will forgive their sins. The water symbolizes the washing away of those sins and the receiving of Jesus' gift of forgiveness.

The next two verses of the hymn are also related to Bible passages that teach the importance and the meaning of baptism. Stanza two is from Romans 6:3–4 and Colossians 2:12. *(Read the verses, if possible).* These passages tell us that in baptism our old sinful life is "buried" just as Jesus was buried, and now we have a new way of life. Stanza three is based on Romans 8:15–16 and Ephesians 4:5–6. *(Again, read if possible.)* These words tell us that everyone who is baptized becomes a child of God.

Obviously the hymn writer was very careful to summarize the scripture's teaching about baptism in every line. However, the central message of the sacrament is repeated at the beginning of each stanza: we are "baptized in water" and "sealed by the Spirit." Repetition in the last line of all three verses also tells us how we should respond to the gift of baptism—we should sing God's praises faithfully, thankfully, and joyfully. So the Bible is our source for all of the teachings of the church; and thanks to Michael Saward we can understand more clearly the Bible's message of what it means to be "Baptized in Water."

PRAYER:
Dear God, thank you for your instructions that come to us in the Bible. We are glad for the gift of baptism that washes us clean and seals us with your Holy Spirit. Amen.

26
Summarized in Song: Jesus' Love

HYMN STORY: "Jesus Loves Me"

PASSAGE: 1 John 4:9–10

PURPOSE: Baptism affirms for each believer the universal truth of Jesus' love.

PREPARATION: Heart. Access to hymn "Jesus Loves Me." Invite the congregation to sing the hymn before sharing the children's sermon.

PRESENTATION:
(Hold up heart shape.) Do you recognize this symbol? What is it? *(Allow someone to answer, "Heart.")* What does the heart shape represent? *(Someone should say, "Love.")* Yes, this symbol means "love." If you were going to think of someone who loves you, your might think of your parents or grandparents, or sisters or brothers. In the church we know whom God sent to show us God's love. Who is that? *(Children should know that it is Jesus.)* Yes, Jesus loves us. We know that, don't we? We learn that from the moment we are baptized.

Is there a song you can think of that tells that story? That's right! There is a song called "Jesus Loves Me." The song was really first a poem in a story written by Anna Warner together with her sister Susan. They both became famous authors in the middle 1800s. "Jesus

Loves Me" was a poem spoken to a sick child in their book *Say and Seal*. The sisters had been left penniless when their parents died, but they were people of strong faith. They taught Sunday school classes to young cadets at West Point Military Academy and used their unique gifts of writing to share the message of Jesus' love. They were both loved by their students and were even given full military honors at their funerals.

Later a man named William Bradbury set their words to music and added the chorus, "Yes, Jesus loves me. The Bible tells me so." With his contribution, the song "Jesus Loves Me" became an immediate success. It has since become one of the most famous hymns sung all around the world. It is often the first song sung by missionaries to new Christians. "Jesus Loves Me" is also a song used at baptism, especially of babies or young children. Yet it is really a song that all of us need to hear, because the message that "Jesus loves us" is the theme of baptism—a very important truth. A professor very knowledgeable about the Bible always reminded his students that the greatest truth in the Christian faith could be summed up in the words: "Jesus loves me; this I know." When we are baptized in Jesus' name, we find that new song in our hearts.

PRAYER:
Dear God, thank you for the assurance that Jesus loves us. Help us to keep the song in our hearts as we share Jesus' love with others. Amen.

27
Symbolized by Sacraments: God's Love

PASSAGE: Mark 16:15–16

PURPOSE: Baptism is a sacrament of the church that assures believers of God's forgiveness and Jesus' love.

PREPARATION: Stop sign (octagonal shape)

PRESENTATION:

What kind of sign is this? (*Hold up an octagonal-shaped stop sign.*) What does it mean? Yes, anyone who sees this shape on our roads is expecting to stop. That's what a symbol does. With one simple shape we create a sign, a symbol that communicates a specific meaning to those who understand it. God knows about the importance of signs and symbols for human beings.

Because we can't easily put our faith into words, God gives the church important signs to offer to people so that we might know that God loves and forgives us. We call these important signs "sacraments"—holy symbols that Jesus gave us to help us recognize God's action in our lives. One sacrament is baptism, when God cleanses us from sin and grants us the Holy Spirit as our guide. Another sacrament is communion, when we understand that Jesus gave his life to save us.

The primary symbol for the sacrament of baptism is water, but another symbol is the shell. Not only did some early Christians use a shell to pour water over the heads of those being baptized, but the shell also represents the protection baptism gives us as we travel through life, much like a shell protects creatures in the sea. Jesus told the first disciples that those who believe and are baptized will be saved. In other words, Jesus told his followers to use water to symbolize that those who trust in him are washed clean from sin and are given new life.

So for the Christian, seeing a symbol for water or the shape of a shell is a sign of God's loving acceptance found in the sacrament of baptism. Just like the octagon, those shapes remind us to stop and remember that we are loved and claimed as God's own children.

PRAYER:
Dear God, thank you for giving us ways to recognize your love. Help us to stop and remember that your love cleanses us like water. Amen.

28
Touched in Love: Jesus' Blessing

PASSAGE: Mark 10:13–16

PURPOSE: A service of blessing recognizes God's special grace and love toward children who represent the relationship God desires with people.

PREPARATION: Sign language symbol for "Love"

PRESENTATION:

I know something that if you give it away, you get it back. Can you guess what it is? *(Allow for guesses.)* The only thing I know of that you can give away and get back in return is . . . a hug! Are you willing to try it? Someone give me a hug. As you wrap your arms around me, I wrap my arms around you. *(Give a volunteer a hug.)* So who is getting the hug? We both are! That's the way love works. In fact, the sign for love is very much like a hug. *(Cross both arms over the chest to demonstrate the sign for "love.")* When we lovingly touch others, we bless them, ask God's favor upon them, and mark them as holy to God.

Sometimes in the church we have special services of blessing for infants and children. Some parents prefer to wait until a child is old enough to choose baptism for himself or herself. However, they still want to recognize God's importance in the child's life and remember how important children are to God. Jesus taught us about blessing children.

Once when Jesus had been teaching crowds of people, some little children tried to press through the disciples who surrounded him. Jesus' disciples were gruff with the children and tried to send them away, but the Bible says Jesus rebuked his helpers—he told the disciples that what they were doing was wrong. Jesus wanted to bless the children, to take them in his arms and let them know how much God loved them. (*Make the sign for "love" again.*) Jesus explained that children show us what kind of relationship we should have with God. He said that in order to be close to God, we need to become like little children. If we "become like little children," we learn to depend on God for all our needs.

What little children do best of all, however, is simply to love those who love them. God offers us unconditional love, like a giant hug. When we open our arms to God, we receive a love that never ends, a love we can share with others. When we bless the children in our family or in our congregation, we affirm the lesson Jesus taught us. Like the disciples, we learn what it means to be a child of God.

PRAYER:
Dear God, thank you for the way you bless our lives. Help us to share the blessing of your love with others. Amen.

29
United by Love: God's Children

Hymn Story: "Child of Blessing, Child of Promise"

Passage: 1 Corinthians 12:12–13

Purpose: Baptism unites us as children of God and though we are many makes us one.

Preparation: Baptismal certificate, church record book. Access to the hymn "Child of Blessing, Child of Promise." Invite the congregation to sing the hymn before sharing the children's sermon.

Presentation:
This is a very official looking form, isn't it? (*Hold up an example of a baptismal certificate, either blank or completed.*) Perhaps you have one like it at home. This is a baptismal certificate. Whenever someone is baptized, the pastor dates and signs a baptismal certificate, and the document becomes a legal record of that person's acceptance into the Christian faith. Baptismal names and dates are kept in a church record book. (*If possible, show the church's record book.*) Baptism is a significant event in a person's life, one that marks the beginning of his or her life in Christ.

But the person baptized is not the only important participant in this sacrament. You and I are important too when we witness a baptism and welcome a new Christian into our congregation. It doesn't matter whose names might be on these certificates, when they are baptized we are made one with them. As we witness the sacrament we promise that we will accept our responsibility to love, support, and care for the infant, child, or adult all through life. Baptism requires us to acknowledge our connection to one another because we are brothers and sisters in God's family.

A contemporary baptismal hymn called "Child of Blessing, Child of Promise" is often sung when children are baptized. The words of the hymn celebrate that each child is a gift from God and in baptism is given back to God. The last verse reminds us that God is the parent of us all, and together we learn to love God most of all. Ronald Cole-Turner wrote the words to this hymn to celebrate the baptism of his own daughter. It is fitting that he wrote it thinking like a parent about his child because that is the way God thinks about each of us. Our job in the church is to remember that God loves each one of us and that we must love each other because we are all united in baptism.

So baptism is a very formal commitment. The church gives us proof of our baptism and keeps legal records of our baptism. It's an important moment. But we must remember too that just as much as baptism is our commitment to God, it is also our commitment to each other—not written on paper but written like a song on our hearts.

PRAYER:

Dear God, thank you for welcoming us as part of your family. Help us to remember that we are brothers and sisters in Christ. Amen.

30
Welcomed in Faith:
God's Family

Passage: Ephesians 3:14–15

Purpose: Just like a new baby becomes part of a family when he or she is born, we become part of God's family when we are baptized.

Preparation: Church directory, photo album

Presentation:
For weeks, conversations at the Wilson household centered on one thing: the new baby. David and Stephanie Wilson already had one child, a three-year-old son named Paul. Stephanie had been trying to prepare Paul for the arrival of another family member. Stephanie had him put his hand on her tummy so he could feel the baby move. Paul caught on quickly, and soon he was talking about "his" baby brother or sister all the time.

Both sets of grandparents were concerned that Paul might feel left out when the baby came, as new brothers and sisters sometimes do. They talked to Paul about how he was going to help his mother with the baby. They asked if he was going to bring her diapers for his brother or sister and if he was going to help pick up toys, because the baby would be too little to do that itself. Paul said that he would help his mom with the diapers, but he wasn't so sure about the toys.

David and Stephanie told Paul many times that they were a family. That meant that they belonged to each other and that they all worked together to help one another. Paul asked how the new baby would help. David and Stephanie had to think about that question for a while, but finally they said, "The baby won't be able to help at first. He or she won't do much but eat, sleep, make wet and dirty diapers, and cry. We will have to do just about everything for the baby for a while. Later on you will be able to play together, and some day the baby will be able to help with things in the family just like you do now."

David, Stephanie, and Paul loved to look through photo albums. (*Show photo album.*) Dad and Mom reminded Paul that they were part of a bigger family as well as the family that lived in their house. "You mean my grandmas and grandpas?" asked Paul.

"Yes, and your uncles and aunts too," said Mom and Dad. "Besides that family we belong to God's family. Just like a new baby becomes part of our family when it is born, we become part of God's family when we are baptized." (*Show church directory.*)

"What's baptized?" asked Paul.

"That is what we call it when the pastor pours water over someone in the church service. It makes us part of God's family," said Dad. "We become children of God. That's a big family. You were baptized when you were a baby and your brother or sister will be baptized a few weeks after birth."

"Will all the family be there?" asked Paul.

"Yes," said Mom. "Your grandmas and grandpas, your aunts and uncles, and your cousins will be there. And our church family too. All the family will be there."

PRAYER:
Dear God, thank you for our families at home and at church. Thank you too that we are part of your family—the family of faith. Amen.

Age-Group Suggestions

Baptism is one of the most significant symbols of church life. Jesus instituted the sacrament of baptism as an outward act of repentance and an inward assurance of redemption. This powerful symbolism is reenacted by each generation as the church receives new members to God's Realm through the sacrament of baptism. Like all symbolic rituals, Holy Baptism may be understood on a variety of levels. Parents, pastors, and educators must be sensitive to the participants' readiness to learn to appreciate traditions and symbols. Use the following suggestions to explore the meaning of baptism with different age groups. Consider a variety of settings and situations that would allow Christians, young and old, to study, share, and learn about this important sacrament of the church.

Preschool: Symbols of Baptism

- Show commonly recognized symbols such as a dollar sign, the golden arches, a heart, and a stop sign and discuss their meanings.

- Discuss symbols that represent Jesus like a church, a cross, a heart, and sheep and a shepherd.

- Display a picture of Jesus' baptism and explain that Jesus gave us the symbol of water to help us remember him.

- Trace a hand-shaped dove and read the story of Jesus' baptism and the descending dove in Matthew 3:16–17.

Early Elementary: Bible Stories of Baptism

◆ Read a story of Jesus' baptism from a Bible storybook.

◆ Draw a picture of Jesus' baptism and add an illustration of each participant to the scene.

◆ Read Bible stories of other people who were baptized, like Cornelius (Acts 10:47–48) or Lydia and her household (Acts 16:11–15).

◆ Sing a song about baptism.

Upper Elementary: Sacrament of Baptism

◆ Read Matthew 28:18–20 and discuss what the "Great Commission" means today.

◆ Look up the word "sacrament" in a Bible dictionary and discuss how the water becomes "sacred"—how Jesus commanded us to use an outward symbol to represent an inner, spiritual truth.

◆ Design a symbol for a poster, a bulletin cover, or baptismal banner.

◆ Read and role-play the baptismal service from the hymnal or book of worship.

Middle School: Terms Related to Baptism

◆ Brainstorm, look up, and write definitions for words and terms that relate to baptism, like font, immersion, sanctification, Trinity, and others.

◆ Make a Baptism Dictionary for study in confirmation classes, Sunday school, youth group, or to share with the congregation.

◆ Create a collage, word weaving, or altar cloth of terms related to the sacrament of Holy Baptism.

◆ Research information about the Jordan River and the Jewish tradition of ritual cleansing. Create a presentation for the congregation or adult Sunday school class.

High School: Methods for Administering Baptism

◆ Brainstorm methods of administering baptism: dipping, immersing, pouring, and sprinkling.

◆ Interview members of the congregation to gather memories of their own or family members' baptismal services.

◆ Collect responses and write a baptism devotional with stories and reflections of those interviewed.

◆ Make a memory by holding an outdoor baptism service at a favorite youth location.

Adult: Interpretations of Baptism

◆ Assign groups or individuals to read background information on theological interpretations of baptism in religious reference books about infant baptism, adult baptism, baptism by immersion, and baptism by sprinkling.

◆ Have each group list primary concepts related to each theory on newsprint or poster board.

◆ Share information by having each group make a report, and discuss the specific tradition of the congregation.

◆ Pray for understanding and tolerance within the Body of Christ; consider visiting or talking with other denominations that share a differing view of baptism practices and procedures.

Hymn-Story
Cross-References

"Baptized in Water"
Sealed in Baptism: Scripture's Instructions

"Child of Blessing, Child of Promise"
United by Love: God's Children

"Jesus Loves Me"
Summarized in Song: Jesus' Love

"Lord, When You Came to Jordan"
Focused for Mission: Epiphany's Promise

"O Jesus, I Have Promised"
Confirmed in Faith: Our Promise

"Savior, Like a Shepherd Lead Us"
Guided in Life: Christ's Flock

"Wash, O God, Our Sons and Daughters"
Promised in Faith: God's Covenant

"When Jesus Came to Jordan"
Empowered for Ministry: Jesus' Baptism

Scripture
Cross-References

Hebrew Scriptures

Genesis 6:11–9:17—Noah
    Claimed by God: Noah's Ark
Genesis 17:1–7, 15–16—Abraham and Sarah
    Cherished by God: Abraham's Covenant
Genesis 17:7—God's Covenant
    Nurtured in Faith: Infant Baptism
Exodus 14:21–22—Moses and the Red Sea
    Saved by Grace: Moses' Deliverance
Psalm 22:9–10—David's Affirmation
    Nurtured in Faith: Infant Baptism
Jeremiah 31:31–34—God's Covenant
    Promised in Faith: God's Covenant

Christian Scriptures

Matthew 3:1–6—John the Baptist
    Called to Repentance: Jordan's Significance
Matthew 3:13–17—Jesus' Baptism (Dove)
    Empowered for Ministry: Jesus' Baptism
Matthew 19:14 – Jesus Blesses Children
    Nurtured in Faith: Infant Baptism
Matthew 28:16–20—Great Commission
    Commissioned by Christ: Disciples' Instructions
Mark 10:13–16—Jesus Blesses Children
    Touched in Love: Jesus' Blessing

Mark 15:1–39—Jesus' Crucifixion
  Challenged to Remember: Christ's Sacrifice
Mark 16:15–16—Jesus' Instructions
  Symbolized by Sacraments: God's Love
Luke 2:25–40—Jesus' Dedication
  Dedicated to God: Love's Response
John 1:29–34—Jesus' Baptism (Epiphany)
  Focused for Mission: Epiphany's Promise
John 3:1–21—Nicodemus
  Cleansed by God: Nicodemus's Lesson
John 3:5—Water and Spirit
  Sealed in Baptism: Scripture's Instructions
John 10:14–15—Jesus the Good Shepherd
  Guided in Life: Christ's Flock
John 14:13–14—Jesus the Living Water
  Gifted for Life: Baptism's Remembrance
Acts 2:37–42—Pentecost
  Filled with the Spirit: Pentecost's Power
Acts 8:4–25—Simon the Magician
  Purchased with Love: Simon's Mistake
Acts 8:26–40—Ethiopian Official
  Covered by Grace: Water's Message
Acts 9:1–20—Saul-Paul
  Changed by God: Paul's Conversion
Acts 10:1–48—Cornelius's Baptism
  Accepted by God: Cornelius's Baptism
Acts 16:11–15—Lydia
  Received in Faith: Lydia's Welcome
Acts 16:16–35—Philippian Jailer
  Released from Sin: Jailer's Conversion
1 Corinthians 12:12–13—Body of Christ
  United by Love: God's Children
Ephesians 1:13—Holy Spirit
  Sealed in Baptism: Scripture's Instructions
Ephesians 1:13–14—Holy Spirit
  Confirmed in Faith: Our Promise
Ephesians 3:14–15—God's Family
  Welcomed in Faith: God's Family
Philippians 2:9–11—Jesus' Name
  Confessed in Faith: Christ's Name

Colossians 2:12—Buried and Raised with Christ
>> *Connected to God: Christ's Resurrection*

Hebrews 8:10–12—God's Covenant
>> *Promised in Faith: God's Covenant*

1 John 4:9–10—Jesus' Love
>> *Summarized in Song: Jesus' Love*

Teaching Tool
Cross-References

Anniversary of Baptism Card or Postcard
Gifted for Life: Baptism's Remembrance

Anointing Oil   *Dedicated to God: Love's Response*

Ark   *Claimed by God: Noah's Ark*

Baby Bottle   *Nurtured in Faith: Infant Baptism*

Baptismal Certificate
United by Love: God's Children

Baptismal Font   *Claimed by God: Noah's Ark*

Basin and Pitcher   *Cleansed by God: Nicodemus's Lesson*

Bible   *Sealed in Baptism: Scripture's Instructions*

Bucket of Water   *Challenged to Remember: Christ's Sacrifice*

Candle   *Filled with the Spirit: Pentecost's Power*

Chains   *Released from Sin: Jailer's Conversion*

Church Directory   *Welcomed in Faith: God's Family*

Containers Filled with Water,
such as Basin, Bottle, Bowl, Bucket,
Pitcher, Sprayer, and Vase
Covered by Grace: Water's Message

Dove   *Empowered for Ministry: Jesus' Baptism*

Fountain   *Commissioned by Christ: Disciples' Instructions*

Globe or World Map
Cherished by God: Abraham's Covenant

Heart   *Summarized in Song: Jesus' Love*

Hose   *Connected to God: Christ's Resurrection*

Ice Cube Tray   *Changed by God: Paul's Conversion*

Kettle   *Changed by God: Paul's Conversion*

"Magic Coin" Trick

                Purchased with Love: Simon's Mistake

Map of Israel   *Called to Repentance: Jordan's Significance*

Matches   *Filled with the Spirit: Pentecost's Power*

Paper Grocery Bag

                Purchased with Love: Simon's Mistake

People from the Congregation
of Different Ages and Ethnic Backgrounds:
Infant, Child, Youth, and Adult

                Accepted by God: Cornelius's Baptism

Photo Album   *Welcomed in Faith: God's Family*

Picture of Jesus, the Good Shepherd

                Guided in Life: Christ's Flock

Pitcher   *Changed by God: Paul's Conversion*

Poster of Methods of
Water Transportation

                Saved by Grace: Moses' Deliverance

Sealed Note   *Confirmed in Faith: Our Promise*

Sign Language Symbol for Love

                Touched in Love: Jesus' Blessing

Sponge   *Challenged to Remember: Christ's Sacrifice*

Star   *Focused for Mission: Epiphany's Promise*

Stop Sign   *Symbolized by Sacraments: God's Love*

Three-Piece Puzzle   *Promised in Faith: God's Covenant*

Triangle   *Confessed in Faith: Christ's Name*

Welcome Mat   *Received in Faith: Lydia's Welcome*

Theme
Cross-References

Anniversary of Baptism
Gifted for Life: Baptism's Remembrance

Blessing of Children
Touched in Love: Jesus' Blessing

Buried/Raised with Christ
Connected to God: Christ's Resurrection
Saved by Grace: Moses' Deliverance
Sealed in Baptism: Scripture's Instructions

Confirmation
Confirmed in Faith: Our Promise

Conversion
Accepted by God: Cornelius's Baptism
Changed by God: Paul's Conversion
Covered by Grace: Water's Message
Purchased with Love: Simon's Mistake
Released from Sin: Jailer's Conversion

Covenant

Cherished by God: Abraham's Covenant

Claimed by God: Noah's Ark

Nurtured in Faith: Infant Baptism

Promised in Faith: God's Covenant

Touched in Love: Jesus' Blessing

United by Love: God's Children

Welcomed in Faith: God's Family

Dedication of Children

Dedicated to God: Love's Response

Easter

Commissioned by Christ: Disciples' Instructions

Connected to God: Christ's Resurrection

Epiphany

Focused for Mission: Epiphany's Promise

Family of God

Accepted by God: Cornelius's Baptism

Cherished by God: Abraham's Covenant

Dedicated to God: Love's Response

Guided in Life: Christ's Flock

Nurtured in Faith: Infant Baptism

Received in Faith: Lydia's Welcome

Released from Sin: Jailer's Conversion

Touched in Love: Jesus' Blessing

United by Love: God's Children

Welcomed in Faith: God's Family

Forgiveness

Accepted by God: Cornelius's Baptism

Challenged to Remember: Christ's Sacrifice

Empowered for Ministry: Jesus' Baptism

Purchased with Love: Simon's Mistake

Released from Sin: Jailer's Conversion

Sealed in Baptism: Scripture's Instructions

Symbolized by Sacraments: God's Love

Gift

Accepted by God: Cornelius's Baptism

Challenged to Remember: Christ's Sacrifice

Filled with the Spirit: Pentecost's Power

Focused for Mission: Epiphany's Promise

Gifted for Life: Baptism's Remembrance

Purchased with Love: Simon's Mistake

Grace

Cherished by God: Abraham's Covenant

Cleansed by God: Nicodemus's Lesson

Confessed in Faith: Christ's Name

Covered by Grace: Water's Message

Promised in Faith: God's Covenant

Purchased with Love: Simon's Mistake

Saved by Grace: Moses' Deliverance

Inner Symbol—Outer Sign

Cleansed by God: Nicodemus's Lesson

Symbolized by Sacraments: God's Love

Invitation

Confirmed in Faith: Our Promise

Received in Faith: Lydia's Welcome

Jesus' Baptism

Empowered for Ministry: Jesus' Baptism

Focused for Mission: Jesus' Baptism

Lent

Challenged to Remember: Christ's Sacrifice

Love

Summarized in Song: Jesus' Love

Symbolized by Sacraments: God's Love

Touched in Love: Jesus' Blessing

Methods of Baptism

Called to Repentance: Jordan's Significance

Connected to God: Christ's Resurrection

Covered by Grace: Water's Message

Name

Confessed in Faith: Christ's Name

New Life

Challenged to Remember: Christ's Sacrifice

Commissioned by Christ: Disciples' Instructions

Connected to God: Christ's Resurrection

Gifted for Life: Baptism's Remembrance

Released from Sin: Jailer's Conversion

Saved by Grace: Moses' Deliverance

Sealed in Baptism: Scripture's Instructions

Pentecost

Filled with the Spirit: Pentecost's Power

Promises

Confirmed in Faith: Our Promise

Dedicated to God: Love's Response

Nurtured in Faith: Infant Baptism

Promised in Faith: God's Covenant

Touched in Love: Jesus' Blessing

United by Love: God's Children

Rebirth

Cherished by God: Abraham's Covenant

Claimed by God: Noah's Ark

Cleansed by God: Nicodemus's Lesson

Gifted for Life: Baptism's Remembrance

Sealed in Baptism: Scripture's Instructions

Resurrection

Commissioned by Christ: Disciples' Instructions

Connected to God: Christ's Resurrection

Sacrament

Symbolized by Sacraments: God's Love

Salvation

Accepted by God: Cornelius's Baptism

Challenged to Remember: Christ's Sacrifice

Changed by God: Paul's Conversion

Claimed by God: Noah's Ark

Covered by Grace: Water's Message

Empowered for Ministry: Jesus' Baptism

Focused for Mission: Epiphany's Promise

Guided in Life: Christ's Flock

Purchased with Love: Simon's Mistake

Received in Faith: Lydia's Welcome

Released from Sin: Jailer's Conversion

Saved by Grace: Moses' Deliverance

Sealed in Baptism: Scripture's Instructions

Summarized in Song: Jesus' Love

Symbolized by Sacraments: God's Love

Sin

Called to Repentance: Jordan's Significance

Challenged to Remember: Christ's Sacrifice

Claimed by God: Noah's Ark

Empowered for Ministry: Jesus' Baptism

Guided in Life: Christ's Flock

Released from Sin: Jailer's Conversion

Sealed in Baptism: Scripture's Instructions

Symbol

Covered by Grace: Water's Message

Empowered for Ministry: Jesus' Baptism

Filled with the Spirit: Pentecost's Power

Symbolized by Sacraments: God's Love

Trinity

Changed by God: Paul's Conversion
Confessed in Faith: Christ's Name
Empowered for Ministry: Jesus' Baptism
Filled with the Spirit: Pentecost's Power
Sealed in Baptism: Scripture's Instructions

Water

Called to Repentance: Jordan's Significance
Challenged to Remember: Christ's Sacrifice
Changed by God: Paul's Conversion
Cherished by God: Abraham's Covenant
Claimed by God: Noah's Ark
Cleansed by God: Nicodemus's Lesson
Commissioned by Christ: Disciples' Instructions
Connected to God: Christ's Resurrection
Covered by Grace: Water's Message
Empowered for Ministry: Jesus' Baptism
Gifted for Life: Baptism's Remembrance
Saved by Grace: Moses' Deliverance
Sealed in Baptism: Scripture's Instructions
Symbolized by Sacraments: God's Love

About the Authors

Phyllis Vos Wezeman

Phyllis Vos Wezeman is president of Active Learning Associates, Inc., and director of Christian Nurture at First Presbyterian Church in South Bend, Indiana. Wezeman has served as adjunct faculty in the education department at Indiana University and the department of theology at the University of Notre Dame. She has taught at the Saint Petersburg (Russia) State University and the Shanghai (China) Teacher's University. Wezeman, who holds a master's in education from Indiana University, is a recipient of three Distinguished Alumna Awards and the Catholic Library Association's Aggioramento Award. Author and coauthor of over nine hundred books and articles, Wezeman and her husband Ken have three children and three grandsons.

Anna L. Liechty

Anna Liechty is a National Board Certified teacher and chair of the English department at Plymouth High School in Indiana. She has also worked as a religious education volunteer, teaching at all levels, directing Sunday morning and youth programming, consulting with congregations about educational ministry, and writing a wide variety of religious-education materials. She serves as vice president of Active Learning Associates, Inc. Liechty lives in Plymouth, Indiana, with her husband Ron, a retired pastor. They have five children and ten grandchildren.

Kenneth R. Wezeman

Kenneth Wezeman holds an M.Div. from Calvin Theological Seminary, Grand Rapids, Michigan, and has served as a chaplain at Ypsilanti State Hospital, Georgia Mental Heath Institute, Appalachian Regional Hospitals in Kentucky, Osteopathic Hospital in Indiana, and St. Joseph Hospital in Indiana, as well as a pastor, counselor, and teacher. Wezeman is currently the business manager and editor of Active Learning Associates, Inc., and the resource coordinator of <rotation.org>, the Web site of the workshop rotation model of Christian education. Coauthor of several books and articles, Wezeman and his wife Phyllis have three children and three grandsons.

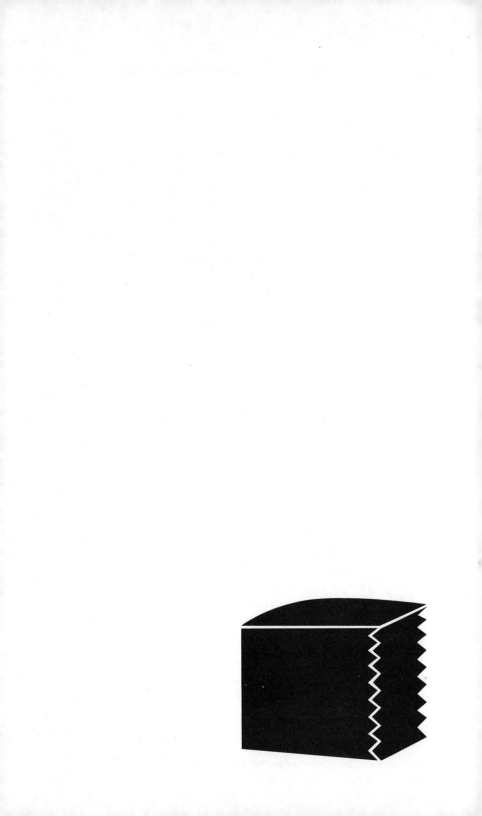